HOMEPLATE WAS THE HEART & OTHER STORIES

_____

BY JOSEPH D. MILOSCH

Joseph Milosch previous books:

THE LOST PILGRIMAGE POEMS

LANDSCAPE OF A WOMAN AND A HUMMINGBIRD

Poetic Matrix Press
www.poeticmatrix.com

Acknowledgement

Grateful acknowledgement is made to the editors of following publications in which some of these stories (or earlier versions of them) originally appeared. *Birmingham Arts Journal, California Quarterly, A Classroom of Poets, Coast Highway, Getting Something Read, Into the Deep, Lucid Stone, Magee Park Poetry Anthology, Nerve Cowboy, Poetry Conspiracy, Poetic Matrix LettrR, Pudding Magazine, San Diego Poetry Annual, Two Cities Review, TidePools, Third Wednesday, Waymark,* and *Weavings.*

Very special thanks to the following people, whose faith and encouragement made this book possible: my wife, Patsy, Glover Davis, Marilyn Chin, Steve Kowit, Fanny Howe, Sue Luzzaro, Gail 'minerva' Hawkins, and John Peterson.

CONTENTS

HOMEPLATE WAS THE HEART
& OTHER STORIES

HOMEPLATE WAS THE HEART
& OTHER STORIES

DEDICATION:

In memory of my wife, Patsy.

ANNIVERSARY

In the shed, George Kell, the radio announcer, said Frank Lary was pitching for the Tigers. My grandfather rubbed sawdust off his shirt and reached for a Goebel's beer. Wood shavings stuck to the hair on his arm, and his palm polished the lip of a long neck bottle.

Nearby, grandmother sat on the porch with her hair in rollers and a spot of gravy on her apron. She shelled peas. Occasionally, she sifted them through her fingers. She judged the smoothness of their skin, the hardness of their core, and the flavor of the soup pea by pea.

When the whole family arrived for their surprise anniversary party, they found her in her rocking chair. Grandmother brought out her picture albums, and grandfather took me by the shoulder. He pointed out his father. That solemn man wore a black tradesman cap.

He said to me, "Someday you will show your grandson a picture of me. Don't forget to show him my father's picture," and above all objections, he gave me that picture of the pie-shaped face with a thin mustache.

Grandpa said about his father, "He came to America. The only thing he could depend on were these," and raised his fists with their two flattened knuckles. Challenging his sons, he said, "I can still strike you boys out."

I knew his stories about Chicago and Western Union. He drove a truck to Detroit from Chicago. On the road he never flashed a bundle of bills, stayed away from bootleg liquor, and he kept an iron pipe within reach in his cab.

He met grandma on the Fourth of July. The corn was knee high, and she watched him fight farm hands for a nickel a round. As thunder clouds thickened and split by lightning, the skin under his eyes cracked and bled.

Afterward, he rinsed his mouth with a bucket of beer. He combed his hair thick with sweat and hair tonic. He accepted a job driving a hay truck. During the harvest, he discovered his feeling for motors and became the town's mechanic.

Grandma taught him to read from parts manuals, how to write, and not to be so quick to fight. At forty-five, I look at pictures of my great-grandfather and grandfather. I remember grandpa telling me how he spat tobacco into the pocket of his glove.

"Tobacco juice is better than Neatsfoot oil for softening leather." Teaching me to cover my throwing hand with my glove, he said, "Don't let the hitter know what's coming. Keep your first two fingers together when you throw a curve."

He wanted me to chew tobacco and make the hitter think I'd spit on the ball. He said, "If the hitter crowds the plate, throw inside. When a pitcher throws inside, you crowd the plate." I remember how he was one of the few I trusted then.

AT BREAKFAST

After working six days a week since the first of the year, Leo arrived home. It was 10 a.m. when he parked in front of his house. Turning off the ignition, he recalled that as a young man he drove home nightly. Nearing retirement, he found that he could no longer stay awake on the daily drive home. Therefore, he alternated the days he stayed in a motel with the days he drove home.

He disliked staying in a motel for two or three nights during the week, nor did he like the way it influenced his 30-year marriage. As he drove and fought sleep, he couldn't stop thinking about the negative impacts work had on his family. When he had pulled over for a nap, his worries about his home-life prevented him from sleeping.

He rubbed his eyes to remove the dryness caused by his fatigue before he lifted his night bag out of the rear bed of his sky-blue pickup. Walking towards his house, he heard a Mexican crooner singing "Mi Prieta Linda" and smiled because it was his wife's cooking song.

It had been awhile since anything made him feel better about being away from home.

Pausing at the side door, he listened to his wife singing and smelled her cooking. Entering the house through the laundry room door, he set his bag on the washer and turned left to walk into the kitchen's doorway. His wife, Alma, stood in front of the oven, grilling serrano chiles.

Beside the comal was a frying pan full of chorizo, papas, and cebolla. "Dame un beso," he said, and she tilted her head and offered her cheek. Kissing her, he smelled her hair, which had cloaked itself in the odors of breakfast. He touched her long brown hair, which was so dark it looked black under the kitchen light.

She tied her hair in a ponytail, and below the long silver feathers dangling from her ears, a few gray hairs curled on her neck. She wore his favorite dress with its lime leaf pattern. He liked the way it exposed her shoulders.

She poured coffee into his black cup with the chipped handle. He sat at the kitchen table. She had tacked on the wall the church calendar and had marked the days he slept in a motel. "It doesn't get any better than this," he said to his wife, who was loading their plates. Sitting down, Alma held his hand, and he said grace.

"Do you like seeing me only on Saturday?" she said.

"No," Leo answered, shaking his head. He

felt too tired to argue and hoped that his silence would disperse her anger.

"What am I to you?" Alma asked.

"Everything."

"Don't lie to me."

"Coming home to you makes me the luckiest man I know."

"Don't lie to me!"

"Why don't you believe me?"

"Because I know you."

"I'm not lying," he said.

"Do you think we'll be together in the next life?"

"I don't know," he answered, trying to avoid the things he had said in previous arguments.

"Am I ugly?" she asked.

Wondering how she balanced her uncertainty about his love with the vastness of her love for him, he said, "You're the prettiest woman west of the Mississippi."

"Be serious. You spend so little time with me now. Do you think you'll spend more time with me when I'm dead?"

Stirring the salsa into his chorizo con papas, he thought because she's been fighting cancer for 15 years, she had the upper hand.

"All I'm asking is for you to be with me while I'm still alive. I want to spend time with you now."

She wouldn't let him take her hand and rub her knuckles. He stared at his food, ashamed to look her in the eyes because he knew in 30 hours he would leave for work and not see her for another week.

He would come home, of course, but she would be asleep when he arrived. When he left at dawn, she would be asleep. Then, there were the nights he slept in a motel.

"You don't know me anymore," she said, "Do you know my favorite color?"

That was her trick question. The answer had multiple choices. When they first married, her favorite color was yellow. The color of the morning flower on a cactus.

Her first cancer diagnosis changed her favorite color to the blue found on the Madonna's cloak in their church. When her cancer reappeared, her favorite color became the shade of the tree leaves above her father's grave.

Sipping his coffee, he looked at the calendar's picture of a California Mission. Below the Spanish word for Sunday, Domingo, was written 1030 mass and Leo leaves at 530. She angered him when she insinuated that he wanted to work out of town.

That anger supplemented his anger with the California traffic that he fought to come home. Also, he was angry at always working far away. He was tired and mad and wanted to say, "Just let me eat in peace."

He considered saying that they both wished to be together; unfortunately, work kept getting in the way, but that was a dead-end comment. Placing his cup on the table, he looked at her and said. "You're right. I don't know your favorite color, but my favorite color is brown, the shade that matches your skin."

Alma looked at him and drew the edge of her hand across her eyes as she quoted his Irish cousin, "You've got the blarney clear up to here." They ate in silence for a while. Rolling her tortilla in the palm of her hand, she said, "Hurry up and eat so you can shower and sleep. When you get up you can buy some beer. I'm going to make tacos."

"Okay," he said and reached for her hand. When she allowed him to hold it and to kiss the back of it, he knew he wasn't quite out of the cold, but the ice between them was beginning to melt.

BEFORE SHE DISAPPEARED

I could say I was in this tourist city looking for art, but that isn't true. I was looking for a poster for my niece as she was about to enter the seventh grade. In the Black Door Bookstore, I came across prints of Duchamp's *Nude Descending a Staircase # 2.*

I could say I thought of that famous poem about Duchamp's painting, but I didn't. I could say that I thought how he drew from the futurists or competed with a new invention — movies — to depict a woman in motion as she took the stairs one step at a time.

I didn't, nor did I think of beauty as a contrast of light and dark. I don't mean dark portrayed as an emotion but depicted as a color like a shadow that the cottonwoods cast along the banks of a desert river. Was it because I was looking for a sentimental poster that the *Nude* touched me?

I bought a poster of a rainbow with unicorns and butterflies and carried it through the streets of this city. As I walked, Duchamp's *Nude* haunted me, and by evening, it started to rain. As I entered a basement bistro, a young woman passed me on the steps.

As she ascended the stairs, the rain formed beads on her hair. Reaching the top, she shook her head, spraying the droplets. When the click of her high-heeled boots became metallic on concrete, her tan coat turned transparent and she disappeared beneath the street lights.

BLAZE OF RED

As a man, I hammered nails on a job-site overlooking Bass Lake. An east wind rose off the waves, off the beach, rocks, trees, and birds rode it in a circling flock. As I prepared to leave work, I wiped down each tool.

I remember Dad finding his hammer in the mud by our fence. He believed I dropped it in the snow. "Hammers don't grow legs and walk," he said, and hands that built decks also tossed me around like a scrap two-by-four.

He had me clean it with steel wool and WD 40. As I worked, he spoke of one Thanksgiving in 1938. His college band played at halftime during the Lion's football game. It was so cold the reed in his mouthpiece split, and he worried his lips would crack and bleed.

Once, he opened his case, removed his horn, and cradled the bell of his clarinet like an ebony chalice. He closed his eyes, took a deep breath, and tucked his elbows to his ribs. He played the woodwind's round oak notes that rose up like the breeze in silk curtains.

I watched him work memories into his music. Men laughed because he couldn't read music. They poked fun at his Polish accent and joked about his glass jeweled cufflinks. He learned to read music and to speak without remembering his native tongue.

Holding my hammer at Bass Lake, I looked at the curved metal claw. It resembled the mouthpiece of dad's clarinet. I remember his eyes focused on his hands as if he forced himself to imagine the route his breath would take through his horn.

His war taught him to teach his son to take a punch and not to teach the boy music or Polish. I pretended to be free from fear as we worked. When he practiced, I watched his eyes follow the last note like a carpenter checking his cut.

Before being drafted, dad accused me of being weak because I didn't live through 'The Great Depression,' unload sacks of grain at thirteen or postpone marriage to fight. As we worked Sandy Beach, he handed me my draft notice, and said, "You will not run to Canada."

With hammers in our hands, we faced each other and stood with our anger a fine line of heat between us. From its wood pile perch, the red wing took off, flashing its red blaze. As we watched the bird, it vanished behind the juncture of pine shadows and reeds.

CREATING THE SOUND OF SILVER

As an old man, Joseph liked to compare playing the clarinet to his hobby. Just as a gardener orchestrates the pure, silver petals of orchids, the musician arranges his solo in such a way that he induces an audience to marvel at the blending of wood and breath.

Joseph said that the trumpet constructed a rapport between the earth and the wind. He believed to play the clarinet one created an alliance between wind and wood. He knew musicians were like gardeners nursing blossoms under an evening breeze.

He played in the house band on a local radio station. As the band leader, he assisted the sound man and created the sound of the horse, Silver for the Lone Ranger Radio Show. To produce the clopping sound of hooves, he slapped the shells of halved coconuts on a board.

To him music existed in his eyes and ears, and he related the creation of a running horse to playing the clarinet. By feeling the wood and capturing air, he crafted crisp hoof beats. Once, the engineer asked him to work on the recording session with Louie Armstrong.

Louie recorded several versions of the same song, and Louie chose one as the master recording. Joseph said, "Each cut was a new record. Sometimes there was a small variation in rhythm. Other times, Louie varied his note inflection, and the outtakes discarded."

Louie and Joseph listened to the relationships the brass created with the woodwinds. Their shared hearing made each cut precious to Joseph. He kept three. He hoarded them in the back of his closet until the day he felt his children were ready or mature enough to listen to the master.

By the time Joseph felt they were ready, his children wanted to listen to Little Richard, Chuck Berry, Fats Domino, or even worse, so many times worse, Johnny Cash, Carl Perkins, and the rest of the singing/guitar players on Sun Records.

Therefore, he listened to Louie by himself, and once or twice, he closed his eyes, which in his solitude became tired flowers in a garden of musical isolation.

DREAMS AND PRAYERS

During college, he became a professional musician. He practiced, ignoring the fear that hung upside down from the rafters. He said, "Music and education are like prayer. All three require a daily effort for anyone to realize any benefit."

Working in the train yard, he unloaded sacks of cement, grain, and salt. Afterward, he rubbed Bengay on his knuckles to overcome the stiffness in his fingers as he fought sleep to practice his clarinet. When he slept, he dreamt of free time.

His efforts earned him an invitation to work in the engineer's booth for the Armstrong recording session. During the session, his eyes jumped from one musician to the next. He became captivated by the spray of drumsticks across cymbals as well as Louie's solos.

Intermittently, Joseph looked at his clarinet's case beneath the table. Occasionally, he massaged his fingers. He hoped for an invitation from the master and prayed that he could remain calm enough to play well.

In the future when he was alone, he remembered the train yard at 1:00 a.m., the smell of lime mixed with fertilizer, and the ache deep in his palms. He remembered his frequent migraines and joked that musicians like bats needed their ears more than their eyes.

He recalled reciting prayers out loud to practice speaking English without an accent. He remembered his room smelling of steam heat and rubbing ointment. To restore to his fingers the agility needed to practice his clarinet, he soaked his hands in Epsom salt

On the night that Armstrong died, he was a middle age man and tired from years spent on the road selling insurance. Listening to the radio, he sat in the chair, located between the coffee table and the window. Hearing the news of Louie's death, he turned off the radio.

He folded the paper that he was reading and placed it on the table next to his cup. "If the average musician works hard, he can create something special once or twice a week. Louie created something exceptional whenever he played his horn," he said. Then, he stood up, walked onto the porch, lit his pipe, and stood a long time under the windless, starless sky.

DRIFTWOOD CALM
Today the Vietnam War Ends —1975

The wind scoured cliff caves clean of everything but wing-flap echoes. As I collected driftwood, I saw an otter break from the brush above the inlet. He leaped wiry and wild from the bank. He splashed into the ocean. Swimming towards mussel-coated rocks, he dove three times and surfaced twice with a rock and a shellfish. Cracking the shell, he ate quickly.

After his third dive, he shook his head and sprinkled the ocean with water droplets. Rolling onto his back, he folded his legs across his chest like a man's arms are folded in his casket. As the sun set, he floated with a driftwood calm before he disappeared among the waves. On the horizon, thin clouds became sun-torched streaks, and I brooded because all this meant nothing to the soldiers who died in Nam.

DZEIDEK

I dig with the toe of my boot through crusted snow and uncover his gray stone. Kneeling, I chip ice with a window scraper from the grooves of his name. I look into the wind. Grandpa, I see a buck in the maple stand at the far corner of the cemetery.

He breaks the snow as he walks. Grandpa, if you could get up we'd shake hands. We'd see the wind drive snow between the buck's legs, and he is as close to me as your spirit, which is quarreling with the winds between the grave markers.

I remember the argument with your sons. You refused to let them place a salt lick outside the blind to attract deer. They said that it would be like shooting ducks, but you wouldn't go for it. You told them, "We're hunters, not city boys."

You shot the only buck from that hunting trip and mounted it on the wall of your lake cottage. I remember the boathouse, the waves slapping the brick foundation, creaking ropes, chains, water stains on the canvas boat covers, and the dust floating in the sunlight.

I recall fishing with you behind the boathouse. We discussed the draft. "Grandma wants me to cut off your little finger. She said that you won't miss it." You reached into your back pocket for tobacco, placed a chew, and spat into the rainbow colors of gas on the water.

You went on to tell me that my uncles forgot how we came here. Great grandfather was in the German army during the 1890s. He came to this country to get away from the Kaiser. The German command sent him his draft notice in 1914.

He threw it away. Now we have a summer home. We fish and hunt like gentlemen. You decide what to do and live with it here. As our eyes locked, you slapped your chest above your heart. Get up Grandpa. Give me your hand, and I will give you mine.

My hand holds a gun as you taught me to grip it. A hand able to intercept the wind, catch snowflakes and allow them to blossom into clear flowers in the canopy covering my blood's creeks, streams, and rivers. Get up, and we'll watch the white tail disappear into the woods.

EVENING SERVICE
a letter to my brother

The wind came thick with fog, heavy with the fragrance of lilacs. A late, afternoon rain falls among junipers and beads on the needles. The bark drips rain. The lawn trembles and I arrive at this place.

As the voice of your death perches on the low branches of the juniper, I park. Drifting in the memory of our camping trip to the falls, I see your arm casting a thin shadow. I recall Trabuco Falls and the shrill call of a red tail hawk.

You said, "I wanted to grow old, fat and use a cane as `Foxy' Grandpa did walking through his small apple orchard." Then, the lone yucca creaked. Its pale, yellow petals had turned brown, brittle, and fallen between the spaces of the plant's needles.

Now the rain darkens the graveyard. The stones form a pattern with the gray bark and new leaves of the sycamore. The swallows nest under the rain gutters of the mausoleums. The birds' songs are small winds breaking from their nests.

I listen to them and the rain falling onto the grass. In this place with its iron arch and gate, I take my place among the pallbearers and grip the wood pole. As I feel the grain, my grief descends like a cloud bank linking needles, branches, trunks, and grass.

I flex my knees and fix my eyes on the diamond patterned cross in the cloth covering your casket. John, my sorrow balls in the soles of my feet making it difficult to walk as we move towards your grave. Setting you down, I am unable to see or remember you clearly.

It is not until the evening when I sit alone at my table and look at the cup, the cream, the spoon, and the pot's cylinder shadow. Then, I am able to see the hawk. It dove for a mouse and knocked itself out against a clump of rocks.

You gave it air through a straw in its beak. You pumped its breast with your thumb as you held it in a T-shirt rag. Unable to save it, you dug a hole and placed it gently into the black soil. We were silent for a moment before leaving it to rest under an oak.

FAR AWAY

We sat in the living room beside the red brick fireplace. As my grandfather lit his Camel cigarette, I saw the smoke stain on his recently turned white mustache. Blowing smoke rings, he began his story. *There is a planet in a leaf-shaped, stellar group, and it is the only one with trees. Their leaves are the shape of the constellation. When the leaves begin to fall, it snows until it blankets the planet. The planet is known for two birds.*

The Metacarpoph Angel is a land bird, and the inhabitants view it as a sin to hunt the bird, whose feathers are fluorescent blue, gold, and chartreuse. The Interphala devil is so ugly that its mother tosses the young out of the nest after they shed their baby down. Because the inhabitants believe every being has the right to eat, walk, and fly, they spread millet in their yards for the Metacarpoph angel to eat and oats on their roofs for the Interphala devil to eat.

When the army drafted me, I remember how his stories made me feel my country was good. In August of '71, I was home on leave. My grandparents visited, and after dinner, we watched the news. Grandpa loosened his tie as he smoked. Dad adjusted his tie's Windsor knot. Grandma sat near the TV in her blue dress with lavender daisies, and mom in her green dress stood in front of the hearth with her coffee and cigarette.

Cronkite talked about the Pontiac Bus Bombing. To stop school integration, the KKK bombed ten school buses. We saw charred hoods and fenders. Next, we viewed a row of wounded in Vietnam. Cameras focused on blood-soaked bandages wrapped on chests and heads.

Grandma turned the TV off; mom placed her cup on the mantle, and dad set his pipe in the rack. Picking up my four-year-old brother, grandpa said, "There is a planet, residing...." As everyone listened, summer came and went with the wind through the window screens.

GENERAL INSPECTION

Dexter, a Viet Nam veteran, dreamed of jungle trees blocking the sky, and the monsoons muffling the moans of the wounded. He was in the Army's drug rehab program and was assigned to help me prepare for a white glove inspection.

Dexter rubbed steel wool over the hooks, holding hammers and pipe wrenches until they were rust free. He taped the shovels' blade and spray-painted the metal. Then, he hung them, and they gleamed black and steel.

When Dexter talked, his voice reminded me of a one-wing fly trapped in a jar. He said, "The Sergeants say that my life is a joke. They think they know me by watching me in the mess hall. They don't know shit. If I hadn't declared myself, the Sergeants wouldn't have a clue."

I told Dexter, "You're an addict. You can't hide shit."

"Screw you. I told you a Jefferson Airplane wasn't an aircraft."

I told him, "Dexter would you look at this tool room. There's not a single speck of dust. If a real plumber or carpenter entered this room, they'd think they'd died and went to hell." Then, a bird's head appeared black in the window's shadow that crossed the floor between us.

Dexter stood with slumped shoulders and looked at the window. I could tell that I hurt him by the flush in his cheek and the way he hung his head. I told him about my dream of playing right-field for the Detroit Tigers.

I wanted to leap high over the right-field fence to steal a home run or throw a runner out from deep in the right-field corner. I told him the truth that my arm had the strength of punky wood then I listened to his dream.

Dexter chewed gum and acted like a bull as he tore the grass with his spikes. He made a leaping catch to show me he could replace the Braves', Hank Aaron. These dreams were as real to Dex as the laughter of medics and MPs on his first night stateside.

On that night, I delivered him in a heroin withdrawal to the infirmary. As the bald M.P. rested his elbow on top of the counter, he nodded at me before he eyed Dexter. He smiled. He twisted his club like a hitter expecting a fastball.

HEART CRACKED AND PEELING

After the doctor diagnosed my wife with cancer, I joined a support group at the Wellness Community. One night a new person walked in and introduced himself as Ronald. He smelled of cigars and his wife stood behind him. Before leaving, she looked at the floor then at him several times. As she went to her group, he said, "She allowed herself to catch cancer."

He came to the group seeking our support for his plan to divorce her because her cancer delayed his college plans. He said, "We married a year ago. It isn't fair." The group consoled him. They explained that all of us had similar feelings, but cancer wasn't a choice. He went for water and never returned. After her session, his wife heard that he left and bit her lower lip.

The next week, his wife joined my performance class. For our Valentine's Day performance, she moved a table to the center of the room. She covered it with a tie-dyed sheet. Taking her tote bag, she disappeared beneath the table. When she called, we joined her under the table. She rested on her knees and elbows.

Wearing a sleeveless white dress, she placed one hand on the buckle of her wide black belt. Her other hand held a heart-shaped candy box against her thigh. He gave her a box of candy for Valentine's Day. Inside her gift, she found divorce papers, wrapped with a red ribbon. Then, she opened the box, spilling six pictures.

She gathered the pictures before spreading them in a fan like a deck of cards. At dinner, he said, "If you don't mind, I'm going to smoke." Reaching into his pocket, he removed his smokes. He flicked his lighter and lit his cigar. He said that he wanted to move ahead and asked for a divorce. She could regain her health. Then, he blew smoke at the baby in the high chair.

She picked a picture, taken on the morning that the three of them paused in front of the zoo. She wanted to cut him out, but he stood in the middle. In the dim light, her shadow depicted hair in need of combing. As her scissors slipped from her fingers, she seemed startled to find a heart in pieces beside her. As we watched her, the air became thick with musk perfume.

Her breathing quickened, making her voice raspy. She whispered that she could save herself if she could believe mornings were beautiful or pictures didn't lie. "See," she said, "We all look happy."

HOMEPLATE WAS THE HEART

He spoke in the broken English of immigrants learning a new language. Perhaps, that is why he rarely talked about the country of his birth, or the location of the farm, or the family he left behind. His grandchildren called him 'Foxy," meaning smart as a fox, but to him a fox was a chicken thief. Thus, he thought his grandchildren disrespected him and asked to be called Dzeidek.

When I was in high school, I threw hay with him. As he leaned on the pitchfork, he rubbed the stub of his ring finger along the handle. He lost it in a harvesting accident. In a way it was predictable that his favorite pitcher would be 'Three Finger' Brown, who lost a part of his index finger in a farm accident. He used his stumpy fingers to create an unhittable curve. Even though Dzeidek's finger remained in Poland, his hand demonstrated the same American toughness that Brown's did.

As we rested near the hay wagon, he listed the earth's nine elements: stumps, rocks, hardpan, dirt, grain, sun, wind, rain, and snow. He compared the landscape of a baseball field to the layout of the farm. Pausing, he looked as if he wanted to say something.

His face changed, and he looked like he did when an unexpected storm appeared before harvest. At that time, he looked into the Huron River's wind. He snarled, and it became the scowl of a thousand ancestors who growled as they faced their enemies coming on horseback along the edge of seasons.

Reaching down and touching my head, he talked about the farm in Poland. They planted wheat in the center field. To the left of the grain, they grew turnips and cabbage. Livestock grazed on the right side, and in the afternoon light, cattle appeared as three-dimensional shadows. An arc-shaped road divided the outer field of wheat and the inner meadows of rye.

The man who taught him the basics of farming drove the wagon along the dirt road. As he went from field to field directing work, he'd call for the men to sacrifice. He meant to work without water or lunch. Dzeidek wanted me to know that a Polish farm wasn't a baseball team.

On Sunday after church, Dzeidek and I would sit on the back porch, which formed a diamond shape with the barn, bullpen, chicken coop, and house around the garden. Listening to the radio, I learned a home run followed the path of memories. I learned that homeplate was the heart of the ball field and the farmhouse was the heart of the farm.

I learned if you worked hard enough nothing was unhittable, not even hitting Brown's curveball. As long as you kept alert like a fox, you could survive the curves that the elements threw. I looked at Dzeidek with admiration because I knew he came to this country and put down roots as gnarled and swollen as his hands.

IF I COULD IMAGINE

In the men's room of a Chula Vista bar,
someone peeled away the decal of a woman
pasted on the red prophylactic machine. Now,
she appears to have a head wound, partly
encased by her undulating hair. The precise
manner used to cut away this decal produced
the sculptured look. This wound begins at her
hairline. It widens until it forms a pear shape on
her cheek.

Utilizing the color of the machine, the artist
peals the decal until it looks like her blood
follows the curve of her lip and falls in drops
from her chin. Gathering into a stream, it flows
across her breast and off the tip of her nipple.
The even lines indicate the carver has practiced.
There is no ignoring her in this place where
light puts the dark image of a man on the wall in
front of him. I raise my hand, covering her with
my shadow.

What metal is absorbing my blood's heat in
this hour when the air holds the human odor?
What lightless fragment follows me as I move

within the community of these men? With the edge of their Buck knives, they try to control the current contained in this woman's breasts. Thus, they can't piss in the company of other men.

I think of the community picnics in my hometown in Michigan. During those occasions, the farm women walked without an escort. Their voices seemed as cool as the man dug lakes. Drinking spiked punch, the men sat in the maple's shade. They discussed their wives, their children, and whose son had the high hard one.

Now men enter this room. One looks at her from the corner of his eyes as he spits in the urinal. He says, "Making room for one more." A second man enters. He looks at her. He says, "You guys better hurry. I got to piss like a racehorse!" A third man enters and looks at her from the corner of his eyes. Four men are fascinated by the mutilated decal.

Men captivated as if she is electric with fragrance and rhythmically taps her high heels. Enchanted by the drawing of her lace dress, these men stare at her savage beauty, exposed in the slope of her back. I know she lives because men preserved her mutilation. I see it by the tarnished tin the blade exposed.

Leaving this bar, I walk to my truck and lean against its bed. The sun is an opaque cup with a blood-red rim. It slides behind the fog as she comes to me with her black eyes and her painted smile. If I could tell her more than it is not make-believe violence, nor is it the men who say, "No harm was meant" that drops my heart like the sandbag on top of the curb.

If I could tell her I envision the cost of being a woman, or I could imagine having my body becoming a day in and day out receptacle of so much need, so much ill-rigged, hitched up dangerously poised lust; she would turn her head, revealing her scar and exposing a feather earring. Then, we would listen to the wind as it lifts her curls into the air.

IF IT WASN'T FOR SOUL

In the past, all my cities had night clubs. In one town, the people who attended these clubs were invisible until they returned to their homes. Occasionally, they became visible at night, but in the morning, the clubs seemed to fade among the liquor stores, warehouses, and garages.

The men wore suits and ties, and the women wore dresses and gloves as if they were going to see the Motown Review at the Fox Theater in Detroit. It was 1966, and only the naïve believed a mixed couple could purchase tickets at the doors of these clubs.

For an interracial couple, there might as well have been a law that prohibited tickets from being sold within 2000 feet of one of these clubs. Therefore, certain club goers were forced to buy their tickets separately.

One afternoon, a sliver of the moon became visible before dusk, and a young man walked with a young woman in a golden dress.

Pleasantly, she laughed when he told her that he would purchase tickets for them at the door of the club up the street.

It was as if he believed they lived in another country. The sound of a transistor radio came from a car parked at the curb. Lee Allen's voice came across the airways. The couple listened.

The disc jockey played Motown and Stax, the Righteous Brothers and James Brown. The man went into the liquor store and purchased a couple of cokes. He returned to share his drinks with her as she weaved in rhythm to the melodies.

As they listened to the music, they danced, ignoring the passer-by who said, "The trouble with soul music is ...," and meant that it was black music. On the other hand, if it wasn't for soul music, the young couple might not have danced in the open as they listened to the radio. After the music ended, they held hands, knowing, I suppose, they might never feel as free again.

In the Temple of Whispers

Finding my mortise tool on the floor by my workbench, my memory opened to that winter day and the whipping I received when dad returned to find his chisel where I left it on the mechanic's vise. "When you stop working, put my tools away!" he said.

He didn't accept excuses for not taking care of his tools. I knew there were consequences for my forgetfulness. I remembered winter mornings. The pine window frames shrunk in the cold. Snow, the poor man's insulation, drifted against the house.

Dad left at 5:30 a.m. with his thermos and a bag lunch. After driving through the counties of farms, he'd return with frozen pastures in his face lines. For fifteen hours, he drank coffee, smoked cigarettes, and drove two-lane roads, which were either paved or dirt.

After he spent his day selling insurance, he came home to a dinner of reheated meatloaf, mashed potatoes, and gravy. He shared his day with mom, polished his shoes before going to bed. After he died, I looked at him in his casket.

He laid with his hands crossed, and I wondered if his strap will forget its looped past and will return to being a belt. When did he decide to use his belt for teaching me `a good work ethic?' We never considered the first commandment: `bulls will be bulls.'

If six of his seven sons love the father will he work with a hammer and chisel in a temple of whispers? I rode with him one night from Detroit to the Sioux. We passed side roads, railroad signs, but there were no signs pointing the way to kindness or hope.

He pulled onto the shoulder and stopped beside a tree-lined pasture. He said, "Thank God for the trees," as if it was a joke only men could understand. We saw a steer with his tail facing the wind. He turned towards us and pawed the ground.

If the cleft hoof of anger battered leaf and bud without thought, how do we learn to stand face to face without locking eyes? Dad, if you stood among the yard's shadows, I'd say, "You thought I could understand you without words. You did what your hands found to do."

"JOE WOULD RATHER TAKE A WHIPPING THAN LEARN..."

Standing in my grandparents' living room, we were about to depart for Ronnie's wedding reception. My dad said to his mother, "Joe would rather take a whipping than learn how to spell the number eight." It was true.

I had taken his beatings for five days straight, and the number eight continued to be elusive. My grandmother smelled of talcum powder as she turned me to face my dad. She gave my neck the warmth of her hands.

She spoke in Polish. She might have defended me or cast an old peasant's enchantment. Her voice could have been the breeze that touched me in sleep with mint blossom fingers. "Spell eight," she said, and I spelled the number.

I don't know why I spelled the word eight correctly, and my dad said, "He does that on purpose." Then, he called me down his hall of justice. "Wipe that smile off your face, or I'll wipe it off myself."

I leaned back into my grandmother's leaf print dress. I frowned. Why did my face say kiss me with the back of your hand? Why did he believe he knew when I was serious and when I clowned? Did I have an odor like the smell of blood?

When my butt and the backs of my thighs stung from his belt, I told myself, "He won't make me cry." It wasn't that I didn't know fear, but the night of the wedding reception I was seven. All night my dad called me to him, made me spell eight.

The last time he called, he was talking to the bride, the groom, and grandpa. I spelled eight, he said, "Joe is like a mule. You have to hit him to get his attention." Grandpa said, "A chip off the old block." Toasting me, he raised his whiskey glass, and my dad lifted his.

Dressed in the image of my father with black wing-tipped shoes, my gray suit, and my light, yellow tie, I felt eight-feet tall with grandpa's praise. I looked at my dad, the groom, and the bride's China amulet. I saw the Virgin painted on the bride's Polish heirloom.

She had twelve painted arrows, forming a small circle in her heart, and her eyes were two Heraldic crosses. They seemed to look at me. That night I raised my glass with its ice cubes floating like human skulls and dreamed about magic rings and swords.

MY BALLROOM
For Jill Moses

The only ballroom in my city existed on a street of abandoned warehouses and shops. This road was always at its ugliest in late February when the gray snow melted into clumps along fences and at the bottoms of trash cans in the alley behind the building.

When the wind stretched brown bags like furs on chain link fences, it was near the end of winter, and the dancehall reminded me of Detroit's Grande Ballroom. I can't forget the bleakness contained in the crumpled and mud stained gloves left along the fence and walk.

In this time of late winter, salt dissolved the ice that plated the entrance's steps. Inside the ballroom, it smelled like an old art museum. If I sketched the dance floor, I'd draw the smoke rising above the dancers.

The cigarette smoke might have indicated a new beginning in the same way that ground fog in March signals the breaking out of a new crop of winter wheat. Whatever it meant, the people inside smiled and laughed. In those days, they called those nights 'A Happening.'

The MC might have called this phenomenon by an old Latin name, which indicated the depth of the beauty that he imagined. If I recorded the sounds, I'd use an eight-track recorder. I'd document forgotten bands like the Bob Seger System or the 3rd power.

To show the full depth of this experience, I'd include the sound of the tambourine played by the girl wearing a corduroy dress. She danced alone, and her footsteps kept time like the beating of a pack of Camels against the palm of a young man.

I too kept time as I watched this dancer with her leather fringe vest and her Buster Brown shoes. I remember her charcoal shadow on the edge of light and wondered if my city would exist if I forgot her milkmaid's hands and her bee keeper's smile.

MY GREAT-GRANDFATHER, THE POLE

With his finger, he dug in the soil of the bait can. Choosing a worm, he rolled it as if judging its weight. Hooking it, he cast the bait at the site where the maple's leaf-lined shadow met water.

At seventy-seven, he didn't say much in either of his languages. He taught me to fish and to set my hook. When he caught a fish, he'd hand me his rod. "Be patient," he said before he lit his cigar. As we fished, he pointed at a group of rocks and the squirrel sitting near the base of a chestnut tree.

During his funeral, I remembered toting fruit trees to him. I dug holes for him. He knelt, smoothed the earth and ground clods of dirt between his thumb and four fingers. He inspected the soil and rolled it. He lifted a handful close to his face.

He tasted the dirt, and the soil tinged his breath already full with the odor of a half-chewed cigar. When I dreamt about him, I saw his hands scarred by hammer and saw. He taught me not to believe in his wife's interpretation of dreams.

He believed in setting the hook firmly into the fish's jaw and in observing its color before filleting it. He paused before eating it, not to recall how the fish came from the rocks' shaded side to attack the bait nor to remember the fish twisting on the line.

He paused to respect the catch. To act otherwise was to disregard his upbringing. After his death, I dreamt that I canoed with a party of men. The trees darkened the river, and the bows of the canoes created waves.

As our wake flattened against the shoreline, the shadow of an owl disappeared into a blue spruce. In the camp a man appeared with a pint and a canteen of water. He emptied the water from my cup.

He poured the whiskey and added water. He handed me the cup as his face sunk into his beard and became the eye of an owl set in a dish of feathers. Quickly, he vanished into the shadows, leaving me the print of his heel in the dirt near the fire.

ONLY DURING THE HARVEST MOON

My grandfather was an Irishman who enjoyed telling his stories about apes in the jungles or wolves in the forest surrounding the Great Lakes. Once he came to visit me when I was in the first grade. I had recently realized that a pound of feathers equaled a pound of rocks and that many of my neighbors' ancestors were immigrants.

I asked him about his parents' country. He replied we came from the northern part of an island where wild geese lived in the woods. It was an ancient place, and our family lived there before St. Patrick drove the snakes into the sea and before the British invaded. Our ancestors built a magical city, and only during the harvest moon would light come to the woods surrounding their metropolis.

It was on that night the high branches of pines sang a song that sounded like dead men moaning because roots squeezed their bones as they burrowed through ancient skeletons.

Before the sky broke into dawn, the moon's light flowed down like breath blowing out of a mouth, shaped like a lopsided O. This happened during the night of the Autumn Equinox when the darkness seemed fragile and faded slowly like the voices of a quartet holding the last note in harmony.

Grandpa said only on this night in this Irish city did this happen: magic became real as the moonlight pierced the blue spruce grove. The pine needles split the light into many tiny beams. Little by little moonlight reassembled itself on top of a patch of leaves sprinkled with berries. Then, the fairy queen appeared with rose red hair and emerald wings. She dropped her cloak, and for one moment she stood in the light unencumbered by shadow and unafraid of morning.

Only when the harvest moon appeared on the night before my birthday did the queen appear in the woods of Roseland.

PEACE ON EARTH

In this city, the old man begins to curse as he pauses at the bottom of the hill. It is early Sunday morning, and he leans on his cane. As he does every Sunday, he breaks his climb to the church upon reaching this spot.

He swears, yet his curses don't fulfill an ambiguous need. They drive his will through his knees. Therefore, his curses act like prayers. He's repeated these oaths for years and wishes his words would drive away his pain like St. Patrick's staff drove off the snakes.

Aging should not make it difficult to walk into the church. Nor should it force a man to need help kneeling on the Prayer kneeler. That is what the old man wants to tell his son when they meet after mass at St. Patrick's pancake breakfast.

After breakfast, he sits in the rose garden on an iron bench. Closing his eyes, he makes the sign of the cross and prays. "Lord, don't let me forget I was born here. I danced here. I married here. I welded rivets in the tallest building. Lord let me remember my family."

While he sits, he snoozes, and his cheeks seem to slough. His hands settle into his lap, and one could imagine him dreaming of legs that are strong enough to stroll over the hills, but it seems clear that his slumber doesn't bring to him a dream of hiking the Big Sur trail.

Upon reaching the state where he stops thinking about his wife's death, as well as his wishing to be free of his pain, he arrives at a point between memory and dream. Thus, he finds his ancestor's path to peace on earth.

PLACES OF THE HAND

As I unpacked your clarinet, I found the pain that has been bothering me like the sun strikes the windshield at dawn. Dad, you are remembered in death. In the third grade, you whipped me for failing to obtain a B average.

I remember the beating I received for hanging tinsel in a group instead of strand by strand. I asked the priest if I had sinned. I told him you said, "Money doesn't grow on trees" as you unsheathed your belt.

I told the priest I dreamed of oak with mistletoe shadows. Today, I caught myself asking, is the promise of death a promise of sleep without memory? Placing your clarinet case on the table, I remembered that the strap was soundless until you snapped it.

As a boy, I told the priest I didn't understand my whipping, and to keep from screaming, I clapped my hands across my mouth. I said, he believed I'd learn respect for money only through fear of pain.

The priest replied, "If you don't care for your shoes, how will your brother use your hand-me-downs?" Some nights my right hand traced a cross in the air as if it longed to move beyond the memory of music and gently touch lips in a whiskered face.

Sometimes I turned my cheek, hoping you'd see. Once, I ran up the school bus steps. I punched out the first guy I saw. I said, 'He made a face.' You said, "When will you ever learn" and took off your belt.

Sometimes you called me back to rub my head, hug me as if you could erase my memory. I remember forgetting my missal; you leaned over, and your belt buckled hissed as it scraped across the back of the pew.

In this memory, I've come to the split, spit-break of burning wood; I've come to cotton-ball shined shoes; I've come to you and your silk ties, your tie clips, cuff links, and rings. I've come to the hard and the soft places of your hands.

I opened your clarinet case and touched the woodwind that shimmered there like black silk, I thought about how you disappeared into the horn when you played. I lifted it and bent as if to whisper into your ear as the first blows of the winter rain landed on my roof.

SATURDAY LANDSCAPE

It would be nice to say I experience a vision of their house, which appears as a ghost-like structure in the middle of this parking lot, but I see nothing, and as I leave, I remember one Saturday in 1950. It is evening. The picture of dogs playing poker hangs on the cinder-block wall of their basement. Beneath it is their old kitchen table with wood-backed chairs.

A small tool box sits on the table. Pliers, two screwdrivers, and wrenches lay inside it. Beside the box a few strands of tobacco form a star in front of a bag of Red Chief chew. To the right of the picture, there is a small window; underneath it stands a steam iron of the sort you will find at the cleaners. The scent from its open lid permeates the room.

Wearing her Saturday babushka, my grandmother adjusts her glasses. She straightens pant legs by tugging the cuffs of a pair of gray trousers. Lifting one pant leg, she inspects the crease closely.

Grandpa sits at the table and disassembles the electrical unit of the broken percolator. While he tries to locate the short, he lifts the Stroh's beer bottle and rubs the bottle's neck along his lips. During the evening, they speak of purchasing their first TV.

The next morning after mass, she wears her Sunday apron and arranges two plates of bacon, eggs, and pierogi on the kitchen table. When he arrives, she pours two cups of coffee. At fifty they continue their weekend ritual of attending church — saying grace — eating breakfast — shuffling the sport's page — clipping coupons.

At the graveyard, I brush the snow from their stones. My sadness is my inability to share their company, and during the spring when the grass turns green, it seems strange that these stones reveal only that two people had lived.

Looking at their names, I brush the snow from my gloves and wonder is it because death hurts the living multiple times: once at the hour of death, again during our visits to the dead that I hear a voice. It is not the wind, coming off the Huron River, nor is it traffic, headed to and from Nine Mile and Mack. It is me, speaking slowly and softly as one closing a nursery door.

SCREAMER
For Pops, who taught me my trade

My first boss was a screamer with his long, hooked nose. After he hired me, he yelled, "Don't be lazy!" He told me I'd always be a laborer or worse a scraper hand. I didn't laugh as he pulled the stakes of my afternoon's work while he yelled, "Wrong! Wrong!"

His wife told me he didn't sing during his morning shower; he cursed Sam, Fred, or any other member of his crew. He claimed he never swore in her presence, but she said he fills the house with the sounds of twelve Harleys, circling the house.

He told her, "You can learn about my work." She disagrees and claims that the number of the rolls of Tums he left on his truck's dash tells her everything she needs to know. At work he screamed, "What do you mean, you stopped because you don't have brakes?"

He would throw a rock at the bulldozer's blade and yell, "Put it in the dirt. It'll stop you!" On the floor of his motor grader, he kept a pile of rocks to throw at grade checkers, scraper operators, water trucks, loaders, or anyone not paying attention to their job.

To those who talked back, he'd say, "If you don't like it, do something -- it's not that you haven't got brains, but you've got to be smarter than a goat." If he got your goat, you might quit or threaten to cut his truck's brake lines or curse him behind his back.

I never forgot his pet sayings: "Driving over your work makes me seasick. It's supposed to be flat and smoooooth. The only time you hit the ground is with your feet, walking to lunch or the head."

Call him hard or a bully, he never called anyone a son of a whore though he'd threaten to hit you with a wrench. When the bulldozer ripped open the earth, unleashing its odor, he broke into dance, stomped dirt clumps, and screamed in harmony with the construction.

SOMEWHERE BETWEEN THE BEGINNING AND THE PRESENT

LYDIA,

As I closed the blinds because sunlight hurts my eyes, I saw the world map hanging on the wall by the window. It reminded me again of Smitty and you. I suppose my problem with sunlight began in October or November of '71. Rain dripped off my plastic poncho as I stood in a formation with those for orders to Nam.

I was thinking of maps when Smitty took the space beside me. Because Smitty was to remain stateside, his appearance startled me, and it shocked us the next morning when we discovered that our orders were changed. I was to remain here in the States while they were shipping Smitty to Nam.

Why they had done it no one ever explained; though, rumor had it someone switched those orders because he was a half-breed Sioux or because he wore love beads. For me this switch was not a joke. As a result, I can work only in dark rooms.

All I know is his plane exploded overseas. On the day of the ceremony celebrating his death, it stopped raining. Then you stepped onto the stage in sunlight, Lydia. The rays reflecting off your sequin purse changed forever the way I react to light.

As I stood at attention beside his casket, one sergeant stood directly behind me. He mumbled, "A good Indian is ...." Later, he offered you his condolences. In the sunlight, the dog tags they presented to you gleamed inside the glass cover. I pulled my cap's brim over my shades. Still, the light coming off the case hurt my eyes.

Lydia, I didn't dare tell you that it wasn't Smitty in the bag and that it was a common trick they pulled. When they couldn't recover a soldier's body, they tied his name tag on another soldier's bag. They knew you would never find out it wasn't your son under the red carnations you placed on the body bag. That we came out of that war changed and incomplete didn't give me the right to make your pain even worse, so I kept my mouth shut and let it ride.

Thinking of him brings this image of you. Dressed in a black coat, you stand in the winged shadow of a recon plane. I wondered what you thought as you touched what you thought was his body, and drops of mist slid off your sleeve onto the plastic bag.

The army taught me the trick of reading a map by finding parts of an idealized woman among its contour lines, but I find it hard to idealize anything. Perhaps I don't want to see anything too clearly. And maybe that has something to do with the fact that I feel lost in daylight, and wear cheap sunglasses in sunny rooms. Often, I sit in the shadows. I close my eyes and enter a place where memories run like rain off hanger roofs and recon planes.

JOE

CIVIL WAR CEMETERY JUNE 6

As Kate waited, I bought us coffee. On the television, a Gospel group sang as the train entered Washington DC. In the college's student center, no one could escape the view of Bobby Kennedy's funeral train, emerging from the trees, lining the tracks.

As I arrived with her coffee and bagel, the young woman leaned towards the TV. Wearing a hint of perfume, she became so rapt with sadness that her ears became red. When the sun dipped behind clouds, we decided to drive along the Huron River.

During the trip, we talked about the war as well as Kennedy's death. Accompanying the radio, she sang and kept the beat by tapping her thigh with her palm. The music lifted our sadness as we drove through the farmland.

A rain shower began as we drove around a curve. Stopping beside an arch of conifers, we held hands. The rain ebbed to a mist. I rolled down my window, and we smelled the pasture as a robin lost its fear and landed on our hood.

The bird inspired us to walk beyond the trees into a field. As we left the pines, we passed the crushed grass where cattle had bedded down. Climbing the knoll, we embraced beside the wire fence.

Plucking a stem of grass, she briefly touched her chin with it. We looked at the graveyard markers, which stood in two rows of eight. The stones blotched with moss. Some rain collected in small linear puddles along the top board of the gate.

Humming that gospel song, she entered the graveyard. Opening her hands, she touched the stones as she stooped to read each date and epitaph. The year 1865 claimed the father and three sons. She read out loud the lines about their bravery.

"To love somebody... To," she sang, stopping to read about a young wife, who died in 1866 a month after she buried her youngest daughter. "She lost her whole family in the same year. It's no wonder that she died," Kate said, kissing the numbers on the gravestone.

Fifty years later, I wonder if our actions were an act of blasphemy. I mean... after we hugged and kissed among the graves, we sang above the dead. We missed, or maybe we ignored the whispering of leaves and grass as Bobby made his way to Arlington.

SUNDAY BALLGAME

In the graveyard, I stand at John's and Dad's graves, watching the ground-fog climbing the ridges of Modjeska Peak. Here, the fog dissipates as time unfurls its wings the color of the sun.

I remember the summer of 1960. We sweated in the grass-tinted light. In the batter's box, I eyed my father on the mound. My brother ragged on me. He said, "Don't let Dad strike you out."

Dad threw hard inside. He thought he'd set me up for his outside curve. As John picked berries in left field, I crowded the plate as I brought my hands within six inches of my belt buckle.

John placed his glove on his head. His shadow danced a jig beside him as he skipped in circles. I dragged a bunt and was chewed out because I did not swing away.

"You should practice hitting not bunting; otherwise, John would be playing third." I had to learn the proper attitude. One time, Dad pulled me from a game because I tossed my glove in the air.

After supper, dad made me wash the dishes to give me time to reflect on my behavior. Dad, I wonder why you needed to strike me out. Why was I required to hit your curve?

I ask, "Why was it so important not to let you back me off the plate?" I learned not to holler when I caught your pitch on my forearm. I learned to take you to the opposite field.

John wanted to practice the piano and not to play baseball. He ended up thinking that he was a Hollywood star. He saw his future fame and fortune through the crystals of cocaine.

After high school, both of us refused to listen to your stories about Charlie Gehringer, hitting homers during batting practice at Tiger Stadium. We rarely visited you. Standing on opposite sides of John's casket, Mike and I became friends.

After we mourned at your funeral, we sat in the backyard as our nieces and nephews played catch. Watching the kids begin a game of pepper, we discussed Spalding gloves, Louisville Sluggers, Frank Lary, and Al Kaline. We talked about our lives as if they were a Sunday ballgame.

SUNDAY—DURING THE GREAT DEPRESSION

In the late evening, the nuns filed into the dining room. My great-grandmother placed a basket of bread and a large bowl of soup in the center of the table. After grace, she served each nun a bowl of soup.

Mother Superior permitted my great-grandmother to share Sunday leftovers with her family. After the adults cleaned the kitchen, they gathered with the nuns in the parlor. The children entertained the nuns. "Oh, what beautiful Irish voices," Mother Superior said.

Mother Superior was aptly fitted for her position because of her absolute beliefs and hatred for foreigners, especially the Irish. "Give them a bag of potatoes, and they will sing and dance," she said often when she believed her housekeeper was almost out of hearing.

Mother Superior knew her cook quit performing as a concert pianist after her marriage. When the Depression arrived, there was no market for an elderly pianist. Why my great-grandmother refused to play for the nuns was her secret, but on Sunday it began.

Mother Superior prodded the children to plead with Great-grandmother until she sat at the piano and played a concerto by Bach, a lullaby, and a pounding tune popular from her youth. As the children danced, the adults clapped, and the nuns politely exchanged winks.

When she finished, the nuns filed into chapel for evening prayers. Great-grandmother adjusted the stove's damper, locked the servant's door, and counted heads. On the walk home, they made the Sign of the Cross as they reached the edge of the graveyard.

Arriving home, they gathered in the kitchen. My grandfather removed his gloves and acted like a conductor as he made a game of lighting the stove's fire with the first match. Great-grandmother heated some tea, and it was time for prayer and bed.

THE BULL PEN

Dzeidek's stories always contained an element of baseball. He wanted me to believe his stories as much as he wanted baseball to be in our blood, but farming was in his blood. When I turned thirteen, he decided that it was time for me to watch the bull mate.

It made mom unhappy, but the aunts said that a woman could not keep her children from growing, and she suffered from the pain of motherhood. Mom said she could not expect much from dad's family because they were farmers, but she acted as if they were stealing me from her.

Then, she taught my brothers and me a new game, called steal a base. "Be sly. Be quick. Think like grandpa," she said as she taught us how to take a base. She wanted us to slide cleanly.

When we were tagged out, she told us to dust yourselves off, to try again. Running the bases reminded me of Dzeidek's favorite story about the Tiger's, Ty Cobb. Before a game, he sharpened his spikes in front of the dugout.

The game reminded me of Dzeidek's favorite Tiger, Ty Cobb. Dzeidek said that Cobb would warm up before a game by sharpening his spikes.

The day came for breeding cows. From Lake Huron the wind brought dark clouds and a threat of rain. As we waited outside the bullpen, Dzeidek said, "A happy cow is a pregnant cow. A pregnant cow is a healthy cow, and women are like cows."

He learned it from the farm manager in Poland, who told him that cows and bulls were like women and men. To select the breed bull, the manager watched a select group of young bucks before choosing the meanest and the strongest to mate. That was why the peasants remained servants. They were bred to be meek.

My uncles and cousins took Dzeidek's comments as a clue to begin a series of jokes about women and men. They thought they were educating me, but I had heard most of the jokes already. When the bull smelled the cow, he snorted, and the men howled.

Dzeidek wanted me to be like Cobb, the greatest base stealer of all time. He studied the pitcher, and Dzeidek scrutinized the Polish farm manager. I needed to know that the runner hid his plans from the man on the mound. The pitcher disguised his intentions from the man on base.

After watching the cattle mate, the manager bragged that he would drink and imitate the bull. My grandfather took the foreman's plans as a sign to run for freedom.

Because the serfs were free in name only, Dzeidek tried to escape three times before he succeeded. His first attempt failed in mid-trip. The manager changed his plans, deciding to stay home with his wife. Unaware of the foreman's presence, my grandfather ran down the road, and the foreman caught him.

His second attempt came during a trip to the mountain to harvest trees for the fences. Because Dzeidek was the best man at swinging the ax, he gave Dzeidek a modicum of freedom. Dzeidek began cutting trees away from the work party. He planned to become lost in the shadows, but the crows exposed him.

After each attempt, it took him time to regain his foreman's trust. He had to be sly as he developed his plan to escape. He wanted me to know that he was daring like Cobb. If given a small opportunity, he was gone. When the manager looked away, he stretched his lead and finally, he stole to America, his new home.

He regained the manager's confidence when his expertise with a team of horses became apparent. Sent to the mill with grain, he returned quickly to the barn like a well-broken horse. His speed paid off, and the manager never caught him dipping into the grain. He was careful not to become greedy and take more than could be blamed on the rats.

He bagged the grain that he misappropriated when he went to the mill. Handful by handful he procured it. During the winter months, the food was scarce, and he sold his booty. As hungry as he became, he remained disciplined at the plate. Thus, he disguised his intentions, and he took several seasons to stash enough money to leave.

During the breeding season, the manager became froggy and bragged of his plan for stealing the heart of a new woman. While the manager followed his dreams, Dzeidek planned to slip away with his satchel, his money, and a pocket full of seed. He was teaching me that life was like a ballgame, and as I listened to his story, my uncles cheered the bull.

The simple story would be describing the bull's sweat and drool, or our excitement as he mounted the cow. A more difficult tale to tell is the one about Mom and me, sitting on the porch. After dinner, we listened to the Tiger's ballgame on the radio.

She wished to know about my experience with the bull and the cow. I wanted to tell her about it, but during the day, a distance further then the bleachers and the plate came between us. For the first time, I realized there were affairs that men didn't discuss with women.

As we rocked on the porch swing, George Kell called the Tiger's game, and I recalled the last ball game I played. In the ninth inning, a runner stood in scoring position. I took a two-strike pitch. When the umpire called strike three, I knew I missed my chance to deliver. I wanted to have that at-bat back as much as I wished I talked to mom on the porch. Instead, I looked at the horizon as the sky darkened, and my mother's sadness permeated the porch like the smell of dairy cattle at nightfall.

THE MUSIC OF A WELL-OILED MACHINE

In late summer, the mechanic, Joseph, pulled out his ballroom record player and listened to his old band's music. On the screened in porch, he danced with his wife.

When they stopped dancing, his wife pinned her braids into a pretzel shaped bun. Then, they fixed dinner and sat with their children in the kitchen. Eating, they listened to his music.

After dinner, Joseph played three records from an Armstrong recording session. He called those discs, outtakes. "Listen," he said, "Here it comes! Here it is! After the son turned thirteen, he no longer watched his father place his records on the turntable. He no longer listened to his father stories about working in the studio with Louie.

"If you ask a trained musician to play an E in the Key of E, he will hit the note. Louie played to an E, and when he did that, he created music." Sipping his drink, he looked out at the horizon.

He rarely talked about engines. He talked about his music. "If a musician is lucky, he innovates like the masters once a week. Louie created magic when he whistled, practiced, or played."

When the son turned thirteen, the late summer afternoons became unpleasant to him. He forgot the importance of listening. He declined to join the family on the porch. He refused to watch the Aurora Borealis, a rainbow strip that shimmered behind the distant islands of Tan Lake. He ridiculed his sister's request to dance.

He refused the music that danced like the distant ribbon of light. He called himself a rocker. He sang the songs of Berry, Diddley, and Domino, and he grew old before he understood. The son lost the belief that his father's stories would nourish him. He never listened to his father play his horn. Nor did he think that he'd find his father dead in the garage.

On that day, the mechanic sat on a stool with his ear pressed against the fender of a running car. He looked as if he were listening to the music of a well-oiled machine.

THE RED WHITE AND BLUE
For the shell-shocked Veterans

I drove heroin-addicted soldiers to the infirmary. These men cried and moaned as they rocked in the front seat of my pickup. One of these men was Dexter, who parted his blond hair down the middle. He wore glasses with circular blue lenses and scratched continuously.

He became hooked after his sergeant gave him a cigarette laced with heroin. When the MP's made him sing 'Take Me Out to the Ballgame,' his voice broke. He choked up large drops of spit hung as if hooked into his teeth and gums. Weeks later, he reported to me.

Dexter said, "I remember you; you drove me to the hospital my first night stateside. You weren't afraid to let me ride in the cab." Every day after lunch, he'd sit stoned in the tool room. He had a nervous habit of fingering his choker of red, white, and blue beads.

He said, "I can stand in front of my lathe all day, trimming, listening to its hum. I love the long, lean note that floats when its engine heats

74

up and whines at a higher pitch." Dexter believed his red beads stood for the blood he left on his work clothes and uniforms.

His white beads stood for what his family and he believed. While we worked, he said, "When I become rich, I'll become a Republican; until then, I will work eight hours for eight hours pay."

His blue beads stood for his bloodline and his family's hatred towards any government agency, including the draft board and the military. He was the son of a machinist and the grandson of the last blacksmith in his hometown.

Dex believed in defying all laws. He'd use drugs and show up late for formation. He wouldn't stitch one corner of his name tag. He was a Confederate, a rebel, and his spirit would not surrender. His choker stood for his defiance.

He believed the needle purified his spirit. His red beads stood for his purification by powder and blood. As I watched the sway of his necklace, he polished galvanized fittings with steel wool. I saw his thin build and his fox-like nose.

Everyone knew about his solo night patrols. He said, "One time I felt a snake or a lizard press against my thigh. I felt it move. It made my asshole pucker," and his face twitched as if the cold, earthy hands of death touched his face. His beaded string gave him courage.

Everyone knew he worked in the tool room. They knew he washed and stacked twenty-four 12x12 window panes with brown paper between them. He cut the sheets so square an eighth of an inch of light could not come between the edge of the glass and the edge of the paper.

All this meant nothing to the mess sergeant who refused him entry to the mess hall unless his platoon sergeant accompanied him.

THE THISTLE

I respected sergeant Bunge because he went Airborne. He jumped in Europe, Korea, and Vietnam. Throwing his legs forward, he walked as if his starched fatigues could part the air like plow blades opened the earth.

His first day in the company, he inspected the cut of our hair and the shine of our belt buckles. *You've heard of Brasso? If you look like a soldier, you'll be a soldier.* Then he cursed, as though it was written in a manual for Sergeants and sweat glistened on his forehead.

He stuttered as he cursed, and his voice seemed to be fueled by anger so deep inside him that he had to pump it out using every muscle in his stomach, back and neck. He cursed, rocking with the effort.

After morning formation, he'd stand outside the hangar door. He would light his cherry wood pipe, blowing rings, and watching them turn into an oblique ring. He'd ask, *Do you support the VC or Jane Fonda?*

He'd asked *Have you read Mao or Marx? Sarge*, I replied, "You wouldn't know a Communist if he had a C branded into his forehead." For this, he took me off flight duty and placed me on the hanger maintenance squad.

Sarge liked the fact I worked all day breaking only for lunch or to have a cup of coffee with him. He wanted me to be serious, to explain my distrust of the Army. He told me his dad was a plumber, his two brothers were plumbers. One died in Korea.

He fought for America, and he showed me the scar on his stomach. He fought for love of his country. He believed combat determined manhood, and he protected his wife. I knew he feared retirement.

He asked, *Do you think I wasted my life?* His urge to question himself made him angry. He wanted his truth set in concrete. Sarge said, *I don't want to believe they lied to me about this war. Were we lied to about Korea? We had to fight the Nazis.*

I saw the camps. The Jews were a living death. Believe me. He told me that he had plastic intestines and that he lived with shrapnel under the scars on his ribs. His career had to have some meaning.

Sarge, I could have joined you. I could have swallowed your myths with coffee. You took me under your wing; you saw in me more than the shadow of what I might be. You refused to call me by my nickname.

Today, I look at the scars on my hand. Each one holds a memory of a job or a year, and the memory of the way I treated you appears in my palm as a thistle that is thin-edged, purple, and stuck beneath a dirt stain.

THOSE WHO PLAYED THE GAME

I learned about baseball as I sat between my great-grandfather and grandfather during holidays and summer picnics. If we were in the park, my uncles and cousins picked an area for the ball field. If we were at the farm, an empty pasture would suffice.

As I grew, I became the runner for the older uncles, who weren't fast anymore. Thus, I learned to play baseball under the guidance of my uncles and cousins. As for my great grandfather, Dzeidek, he learned baseball as he came across the ocean in the late 1890s.

Nothing on the ship reminded him of the farm except for the sun, which burned over the water as merciless as it did over land. His village miller said the ocean sparkled like a jewel, but to Dzeidek, the sea was an ugly green. He didn't know anything about Wee Willie Keeler or 'Tinker to Evers to Chance.' A Lithuanian sailor spoke Polish. With Dzeidek he discussed the greenness of the Polish plains as well as the time it took for the ship to travel nine leagues.

The Dutch Cringle was the first knot the sailor taught him to tie. Then, the Lithuanian instructed Dzeidek on the Dutchman, Honus Wagner. Besides becoming proficient with hook and tackle, he learned that the nip was the part of the knot that applied pressure.

The Lithuanian said that tying knots was like pitching a baseball. One needed to know where to apply pressure to control the knot or to make the ball curve like 'Three-Finger' Brown. He learned that 'Three Finger' Brown lost part of his finger in a farming accident; Wee Willie Keeler swung the ax, Tinkers, Evers, and Chance turned double plays that broke the hearts of Giants, and the Georgia Peach was the best at stealing second base.

The Lithuanian sailor told stories about strange animals in the new world. The Canadians called one fowl the Gammy Bird, and the seafowl gathered like ships passing at sea. They traded news by quacking sociably. Americans acted like Gammy birds. After a ballgame, they gathered in taverns to gab about baseball.

During the day, Dzeidek coiled rope as the deckhand taught him. In the evening, the Lithuanian and the immigrant boys arranged the coils into an outline of a diamond on the foredeck. He called the rope coils: first base, second base, third base, and home. Yelling 'Home run!' the boys chased each other around the bases, and a 'homer' was the first English word Dzeidek learned.

Next, he learned to count to nine in English because that was the number of players on a team and innings in a game. The magic contained in the number nine surpassed only by the magic in the names of Cobb, Keeler, Brown, and Wagner.

Dzeidek learned that right field stood to the right of the center field flag pole, located in the center of the outfield and before playing a game, the pitchers warmed up in the bullpen. This knowledge gave him confidence, and knowing the infield was between home plate and the outfield made him proud.

They crept past the islands south of Sweden and Norway. Slowly, they sailed past the tip of Denmark. Time dragged during their stop in Amsterdam, and their passage through the English Channel. Finally, the continent faded beneath the horizon.

The night's air cooled and soothed his sun blistered lips. He liked the stars, and they seemed bigger and brighter than the ones over the barnyard fence. As he listened to baseball stories, he helped his friend sew patches on the canvas bags and learned to stitch a baseball.

He learned American jargon because the Lithuanian told him that the knowledge of baseball allowed him to become an American. By the time, the ship docked at Ellis Island, he knew they made baseballs from cowhide and to catch a pop up is as easy as catching a can of corn.

I remember sitting beside my great grandfather in the tack room. "I saw Cobb play," he said, "Before a game, he sat in front of the dugout. Sharpening his spikes, he imagined stealing his way around the base paths. When I sharpened my tools in Poland, I imagined running until I reached my new home. You could learn from Cobb. Be strong. Be mean."

I read him the box scores as he rubbed Neatsfoot oil into his leather harness. Horses had gone the way of Cobb's exploits. Still, he showed me how to stitch cowhide. "One day the car will go away; then, you will be happy I taught you how to mend harness," he said.

"One day," he repeated as if knowing for me to escape the factory, I needed to remember the smell of rawhide and Cobb's exploits. He believed that his knowledge would allow me to build a home in a land where the horse was king, and the men gathered in the taverns to discuss the heroics of those who played the game.

WINTER RAIN

Tracing the cutting board's wood grain contours, I draw a map. Clumps of dough become the mountains that we rode through. The dark spot is Fresno. The knot is Yosemite; the bluish grey smoke appears around my brother's exhaust pipes.

I follow the round metal echoes of his pipes. I watch him slice a low cloud and slip in the curve. His hands grasp for a hold. He spills, and his knees fling rocks. He straightens then buckles into the berm.

I stand looking at the water running in small streams around his neck and arms. I want him to get up and scream at the black specks rising between treetops and clouds. I want him to stand his bike up, clean mud from the frame, and share a chew of Red Chief with me.

Derek, I keep your death on a peninsula of my heart. It is there that I keep the rock outcrop, the trees, and the crows, who circled on the upslope breeze. On its beach, I keep the wind burn markings on your cheek, your chin's flat leaf scar, and your winged-eel tattoo.

Standing in the first winter rain, I want to release memories of you on the wind that rises inside me as much as when we made a gloved cross on your casket. At that time I wished to open the lid and receive a glance from your eyes.

AUTHOR BIOGRAPHY

Joe Milosch was born in 1947 in Detroit, Michigan and formally educated in the public schools and at San Diego State University. He has multiple nominations for the Pushcart and received the Mira Costa College Excellence in Literature award. He won the Tennessee Middle State University Chapbook Award and the Hackney Literary Award. He was the First Runner-Up for the Steve Kowit Award, a Semi-finalist in the 2018 Pangaea Prize for Poetry, and a finalist in the Tennessee Middle State University Chapbook Award.

His books of poetry are *The Lost Pilgrimage Poems* and *Landscape of a Woman and a Hummingbird.*

www.ingramcontent.com/pod-product-compliance
Lightning Source LLC
Chambersburg PA
CBHW051432090426
42737CB00014B/2943